Louise Pagé

The Man behind the Dancing Bear

2018

ISBN: 978-2-9817545-1-6

This book is a condensed version of a book originally published by the author in French in 2016: Montreurs d'ours de l'Ariège à l'Amérique ; 1874-1914, Éditions GID.

Complete references and more material can be found at: https://leseditionsgid.com/montreurs-d-ours-de-l-ariege-a-l-amerique-1874-1914.html

Photo on cover:

Young man and his animal, Arundel, England. Circa 1890.

Source: Wikipedia.

* Inhabitants of a French Department located in the central Pyrenean area south of France adjacent to Spain border.

To Mary Lou Decossaux

(1957–2011)

descendant of Jean BROUÉ Samsou

Acknowledgments

Research like this one is unthinkable without the support of many people. Frequent exchanges with Françoise Lewis of Montreal, the late Jean-Louis Deschamps and Pascal Gentié of Ariège, helped anchor my story in the real world. I thank them for their help as well as for their friendship. Thank you also to all the members of the Quebec and Ariège historical societies, mayors and staff of the Ariège villages.

A big thank you to André Rocque for the English translation of the book and a special thanks to Daniel and Pierre Tourigny who read the manuscripts and offered constructive comments.

Introduction

BROUÉ — ROGALLE — The Bear —The Boat.

It is in this order that my mother Madeleine BROUÉ narrated the arrival of her grandfather Jean BROUÉ towards the end of the nineteenth century.

Jean BROUÉ, a Frenchman from the Pyrenees, arrived in America with his friend ROGALLE and a brown bear from the Pyrenees. Their occupation was bear performers.

Is this story true? How can we distinguish the truth from the fantasy? The rarity of documents makes this story hard to believe in a family where oral tradition dominates the written word. One document, the marriage certificate of Jean BROUÉ in Saint-André-Avellin, Quebec in 1890, a few rare photographs and anecdotes from my mother served as benchmarks to trace the unusual story of my ancestor's life.

After five years of thorough research in Quebec, New York State and France, the life story of this immigrant bear performer has emerged and revealed a busy and unusual life.

Studying the only available document, the marriage certificate of Jean BROUÉ in Saint-André-Avellin with Philomène GAUTHIER in 1890, reveals a little of his history. He was from Oust in the Pyrenees and his parents were Pierre BROUÉ and Marianne COCHE (misspelled). Her surname was in fact CAU.

Although his age is not given in the marriage certificate, it was quite easy to identify him, since the civil status records are available for consultation at the town hall of Oust in Ariège in the French Pyrenees. A local genealogist undertook a first research. Jean BROUÉ Cabillot, son of

Pierre BROUÉ Cabillot and Marianne CAU Ramoun known as Cabillot, was born on September 22, 1865, under the French Second Empire in Arrous, a hamlet in the heights of Oust. His friend Alfred ROGALLE Péou was also of Arrous.

Knowing the date of birth and his nickname Cabillot allowed the adventure to begin. It turned out that this book, which was to be the story of this immigrant Jean BROUÉ Cabillot, carried me to an unsuspected world and it became the story of all these men – and one woman– who transformed their life by "showing" a bear.

One of the greatest discoveries of this research was merely to realize that traveling with a bear was not as exceptional as it first seemed. Indeed, several men of Ariège decided to leave their hamlets to come to the Americas. Ninety-three of them arrived at the ports of Québec City and Montreal from Liverpool, Glasgow and Belfast. They are presented in order of arrival of the twenty-seven ships which carried them between 1874 and 1914.

Ariège, 09 department

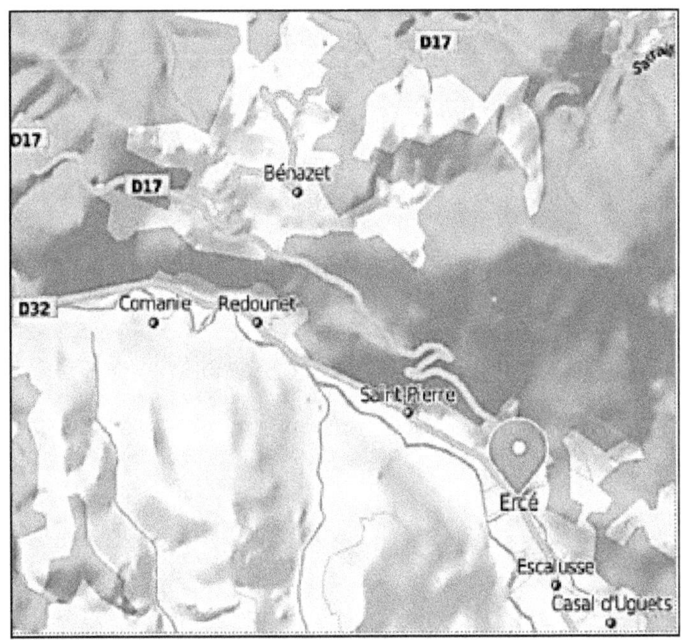

Ercé and the neighboring hamlets in the French Pyrenees

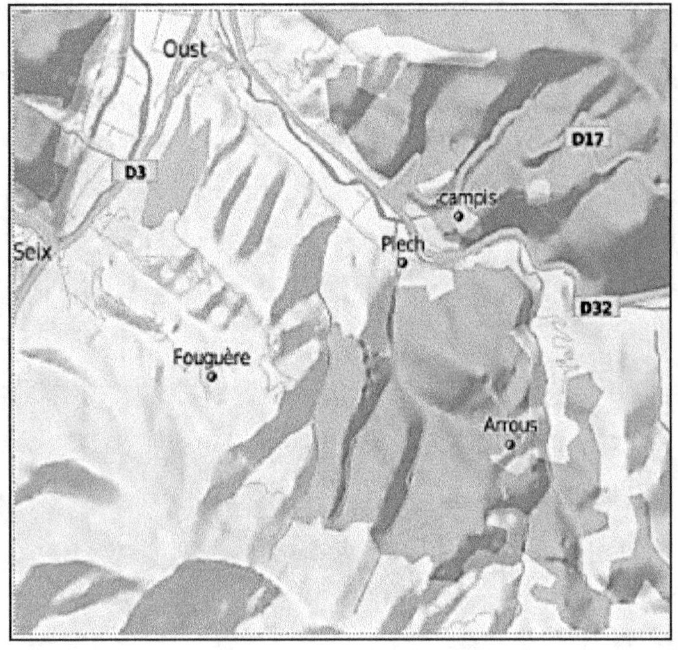

Oust and the neighboring hamlets in the French Pyrenees

Chapter 1

The bear performers from Ariège

In the 1860s, a potato blight famine forced the peasants of Ariège, a department in the French Pyrenees region, to migrate to find work. Life in these high mountain hamlets became particularly difficult and the inhabitants demonstrated their creativity to get by and to dream of a better future.

Notably, there was the development of trades that forced many men and some women to travel; southbound they went on the roads leading to Spain, or northbound towards the Gers and Lot-et-Garonne departments. These trades consisted in haying, harvesting and even selling sheep cheese.

In 1858, Bernadette Soubirous recounted her visions of the Virgin Mary at Massabielle Grotto in Lourdes and a religious fervor followed, which attracted pilgrims from everywhere. Vendors and showmen recognized a good opportunity when they saw one and gypsies could be seen traveling in caravans with women and children and bears and monkeys. They set up camps in the Pyrenees, the men showed bears and monkeys, while the women begged with the children.

These show people inspired our resourceful Ariégeois also to show bears. Activity began in the valleys of Alet and Garbet, specifically in Ustou where it already existed, but as an individual activity. BARDOU, CAZAUX, AMILHAT, SOUQUÉ and many others captured orphan cubs in the surrounding mountain and trained them to perform in road shows. The trade spread to other villages, Oust, Ercé and Aulus. The activity became so extensive that in 1863 the French Minister of the Interior directed the prefectures to create a registry of showmen based on "Carnets de saltimbanque" (busker's notebook).

Indeed from then on, in order to perform on the streets and public squares, it was made compulsory for the showmen to acquire this notebook and get it stamped at the town halls of the cities visited. Because of this mandatory requirement and the personal information it contains on the performers, the registry, which can be consulted in the departmental archives of Ariège, has become an essential databank for this book.

During the fifty years of existence of this registry, 515 permits were issued to bear performers, 95% of whom were from Ustou, Ercé and Oust in Ariège, and the rest mostly to foreigners from Turkey (notably from Constantinople), Bosnia and Italy. There was competition, but soon they began to travel around the world. From the Pyrenees and bordering countries, they suddenly find themselves exploring the possibility of living in South America, New Orleans and New York.

It was only in 1871 after the Franco-Prussian War that three performers and their bears landed in New York. They had left their hamlet Cominac, walked to Boussens, fifty kilometres away, and from there, along the rail line to Le Havre stopping in each village to earn money to travel to England, a journey of about 850 kilometres. In the neighborhood of Le Havre, they took a boat that accepted them with their animals. In England, still following the rails so as not to get lost, they showed the bear on the way, a journey of 300 kilometres. These first bear performers went to Scotland, and from Glasgow took a ship to New York. They stayed in North America only one season and returned to their village. In the story of their adventures and especially at the sight of their full purse, others imitated them and so began the North American adventure of the bear performers.

In Canada, it was not until 1874 that these temporary migrants arrived in Québec City. French Canada was not well known to them because the ties of Canada with France, broken by the Conquest of 1763 by England, had not resumed until 1855.

The re-establishment of links between France and Canada allowed the captains of the commercial lines between Liverpool and the ports of Quebec Province to carry French migrants. Ariègeois bear performers no longer had to go through the United States to come to Canada. They discovered themselves naturally attracted to Quebec because of the French language that they spoke fluently, even though their mother tongue was Occitan. Another factor attracted them: it was easier to enter the United States by land rather than to arrive directly in New York City via Castle Garden and from 1892 on, via Ellis Island. These two ports of entry for immigrants were merely imposing more formalities.

The arrival of Frenchmen on commercial lines between England and Canada is listed in the passengers' lists from 1865. The consultation of the ships manifests and lists of passengers that arrived at the ports of Québec City and Montreal allows the identification of the bear showmen from Ariège.

The transatlantic ships mentioned in the various chapters of this book belong to Anglo-Canadian companies that regularly traveled between England and Canada. One will notice the fleets of the Beaver Line which owned the LAKE CHAMPLAIN, LAKE ERIE, LAKE HURON, LAKE MANITOBA, LAKE NEPIGON, LAKE ONTARIO, LAKE SUPERIOR, RUAPEHU and LAKE WINNIPEG; the Dominion Line, a Canadian company established in 1867, which included: MONTREAL, TORONTO and BROOKLYN steamships while in the Allan Line one can find the following ships: BUENOS AYREAN, CORINTHIAN, GRECIAN, PERUVIAN, SARDINIAN and SIBERIAN; and in the American Line, the ships: PHILADELPHIAN and SARMATIAN.

All these steamships (SS) did accept on board in steerage some animals and even bears, of course, with constant supervision by their masters. The Atlantic crossing had lasted between nine and twenty-one days depending on the weather conditions. Some of these ships, which left early in April or late in November, collided with icebergs or remained trapped in the ice, causing breakage and delays. Some bear performers have made the crossing in more than difficult conditions as you will discover in the next chapters.

Moreover, no one will be surprised to know that to bind one's life to that of a bear is not without risks. Even though they tamed the animals very soon after their births, some showmen have died under the claws of their livelihood or in the exercise of their craft. An element to meditate for anyone who would like to engage in this very special art.

However it is fair to say that, generally speaking, the people they met on their journey in various places had loved this kind of show, which consequently motivated the bear performers and helped them fill their purses.

The Bear

The bear trained by the performers is brown and often called the cinnamon bear. It has pretty rounded ears and a bump of fat on the back of its neck. It stands naturally on its hind legs and can stay for some time in this position while its handler is directing it to do so using a stick called the "bastoun" in Occitan.

From the Ursus Arctus family, its back forms a bow when it is standing up. In the 1850s, this bear was abundant in the Pyrenees and its hunting was strongly encouraged by the authorities and farmers. There was even bear steak to be consumed in restaurants.

The first trained bears were cubs left by hunters. The Pyrenean bear is gentler than its Canadian cousins. It is smaller and does not hibernate completely in winter. Winters in Ariège are not as rigorous as the Canadian winters, so in Ariège, the bear establishes several dens, and is sleepy rather than completely asleep. This explains that the bear handler could move somewhat in November and December before putting their pet up in a boarding stable.

In order to reduce the aggressiveness of the males, they were castrated at a very young age. The village butcher took charge of this task. A castrated animal was becoming larger, an effect sought in this trade.

Moreover, as the master had to instruct the bear to dance, to sit on a stool or to get down on all four paws, the tradition that goes back to very old times was to put a ring in the muzzle of the bear and to attach a chain that the master manipulated according to the orders he wanted to give. This technique is called "ferrade".

While on tour, the bear usually wore a covering leather muzzle and a leather collar around its neck, which was used to leash it for a walk or to tie it to the master's house.

The butcher also took care of declawing the animal, but the claws would grow back and could then become dangerous. A vigilant master would regularly file down the claws of his protégé; you will see in the photographs that some bear performers neglected this part of the maintenance of the animal.

All these techniques appear barbaric to today's eyes, but they were carried out in respect of the animal (after all, it was their livelihood) and the bear tamer waited until it was completely healed before proceeding to train the animal. When the Pyrenean cub supply ran out in the 1890s, the bear masters bought Balkan cubs delivered to the port of Marseille. These bears were of the same family as the Pyrenean bears, but smaller in adulthood and with less shiny hair.

Because bears are omnivorous animals, it was relatively easy to feed them in captivity and on the road. They ate mainly table scraps and berries gleaned en route. The trained bear, well looked after by its master, had a life expectancy of about fifteen years. Those living in the wild lived less long for being hunted. This hunt was strongly encouraged in Ariège in those years for protecting the cattle.

When the bear performer was at home in Ariège, the animal was lodged in the "soutou" on the ground floor of the house, and when the weather was nice, it was tied outside to a ring firmly anchored in the wall of the house. On the move, it lodged in a barn, still tied up and away from the horses or restrained to a ring outside. It could also stay in winter boarding in zoos like the Central Park zoo in New York City.

Typically, the show staged by the master consisted of the imitation by the bear of the shepherd wandering with the "bastoun" in the fields, also there were commonly a mimic of the dance of the young ladies to the sound of a lively music to Occitan onomatopoeia, the affective kiss to his master and other drolleries. In America, bear performers added a scene where the bear sat on a stool and another in which the bear climbed up a pole.

The master began to show his bear as soon as it turned one. At first, it was skinny, but it quickly gained weight.

The Bear Dance

e-roun toun toun lari-loularila—lari lariletto—larilette—e-roun toun toun lari-lou larila—lari larilletto—eroun toun la.

The man

The bear performers who came to Quebec were born between 1830 and 1880, almost all Ariégeois. There were also some Turks who came with a wife and children, bears and monkeys; they appear in the description of arrivals at the ports of Québec City and Montreal.

Bear performers whose biography you will read in the next chapters come mainly from the villages of Oust and Ercé (see map at the beginning of the book).

Military service was an important part of the lives of these men. At the age of 20, they were expected to serve for three years and thereafter perform three short periods of training. Bear performers began their travels after their service, but there are some exceptions.

Oust and the hamlet of Arrous

The village of Oust runs along the Garbet River and extends over several satellite hamlets far from the centre and located in the heights of the Pyrenees. Access to these hamlets is not easy, and most of the communication was done on foot at the time of the bear performers. These hamlets with colorful names such as Arrous, Miramont, Perteguet, Plech and Roume, are located on both sides of the Garbet River. The hamlet most often mentioned in this book is Arrous. It is an old hamlet, sheltering at its peak a 120 people in 24 houses set close to each other to protect them from the wind and cold at these heights. An owner could own several plots of land. Its inhabitants grew cereals and owned some cows and sometimes a donkey. In Arrous, there is a fountain to get drinking water and a flour mill that was built by François BROUÉ Cabillot. The first bear performer to set foot in Quebec in 1874 was Jean BROUÉ Samsou d'Arrous. He thus inaugurates in Quebec the story of an industry that will last forty years.

The territory of Arrous is extremely fragmented as evidenced by the land record of 1670.

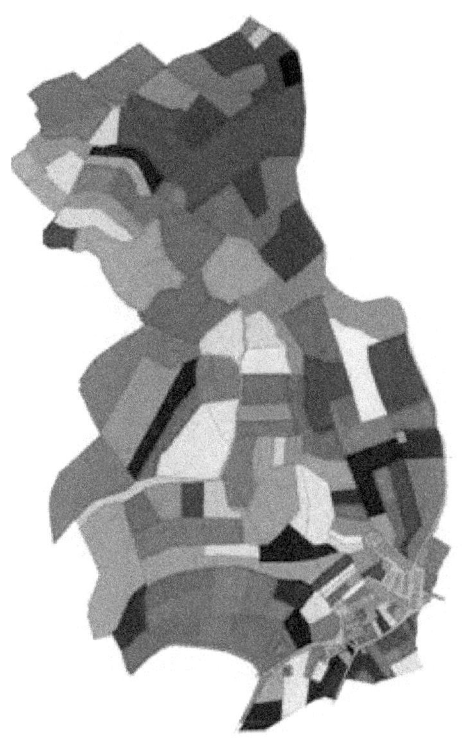

Ercé and its hamlet of Cominac

Ercé is famous for its bear performers, the "bear dens" and its "school for bears". Eighty percent of the bear performers who came to Quebec were from Ercé, some from the village itself and the others from the constellation of tiny hamlets surrounding it. For the record, they are Cominac, La Rivière, Comanie, Goulos, Las Costes, Escalanère, Bout-du-Village, Benazets, Camp Subra, Courtiou de Faoure, Courtiou de Rouze, Escalusse, Espouex, La Carole, Le Carré, Labouche and Trounet.

By the way, it was at Cominac that one of the most bizarre anecdotes relating to the separation of Church and State (a law passed in 1905) and the presence of bear performers took place. One day, the priest CAUJOLLE, protected by a "bears" guard of honor conducted by some parishioners, had walked up to the front of his church to read a letter of protest concerning the inventory of the cult objects which was imposed on him, once they arrived the civil servants in charge of the case seeing these impressive bodyguards became frightened and left at once! The task could not be accomplished before the following year... The reason invoked to oppose the inventory was that the construction of the church had been financed by the parishioners and that the State was misappropriating their property.

It is also Cominac that will contribute to the boom of the bear show business. There is now in Ercé a museum of bear performers named "Espace des montreurs d'ours". There are objects used in the trade: the muzzle, the "bastoun", the costume and panels telling the story of these bear performers.

Another museum, the "Museo degli orsanti", is dedicated to Italian bear performers in Compiano, Italy.

The importance of sobriquets in Ariège

To perform genealogical and historical research in Ariège, knowledge of the surname is essential, but not enough. As will be seen below, my ancestor Jean BROUÉ had an uncle named Jean BROUÉ, a half-brother also named Jean BROUÉ and at least three cousins of the same name as well. The sobriquet, a nickname, then becomes useful to distinguish them. The uncle is Jean BROUÉ Samsou, the half-brother Jean BROUÉ Cabillot of Couflens and the cousin Jean BROUÉ Cabillot Pétiou. When a sobriquet does not distinguish individuals, a second or even a third is added. These nicknames are in Occitan patois, as we have seen, a mixture of French, Latin and Spanish. The nicknames refer to physical characteristics—Samsou is Samson (name derived from the biblical strongman), Pétiou is small and Cabillot is apparently a derivative of Cabilhou, a wooden peg or the dried corn cob that was used to insulate houses.

In these Ariège villages, the social organization revolves around the house. The sobriquet becomes the name of the house. The house is passed on to the eldest of the boys in the family, and he continues the sobriquet. His brothers, who have no right to the inheritance, must move to their wives' houses if they are "endowed" and thus inherit another sobriquet. The women changed their names in marriage, but keep their original surnames in the notarial deeds and on their death certificates.

The bear performers who were hired in circuses or who worked in Dime Museums took names like Capt'n Cardona (Jean Pierre DEGEILH Malet) or Capt'n Ricardo (Joseph ANDREU Pascoualet).

The bear performer and his travels in North America

Once in Québec City or Montreal, the bear performers had the choice of working in the area or leaving immediately for the United States, specifically, the State of New York. Their decision depended on the time of year. In general, they spent the summer in Quebec and went south in September.

The Ariégeois did not like sleeping under the stars very much; they did it only in case of necessity. They preferred to stay at an inn or in a small hotel often held by French people who welcomed them with the bear. In the 1880s, those who arrived at the Port of Montreal probably went to Old Joe's Beef Tavern in Old Montreal. Owner Charles McKiernan was known for his generosity, and the bears he housed in the basement helped him maintain order in his hotel. In the 1890s, Maurice DURRACQ from Sabres and his wife Maria ROGALLE Clar from Cominac operated a hotel with restaurant called Hotel Commercial. It was located on Notre-Dame Street West on the left of the Corona Theatre (Family Theatre in the 1890s). The meeting place for Montreal bear performers was born.

In New York City, bear performers initially lodged at the Paris hotel or in rooming houses. Some Bear performers who accumulated a nest egg started small hotels. So we saw the PERTHUS hostel, the POUECH inn and the PEYRAT hotel. These inns are frequently mentioned as places of residence of the Ariégeois in New York in the lists of passengers of ships.

These innkeepers played a big role in the life of the Ariège diaspora in America. They transmitted messages, gave news of the bear performers and provided work for some during the winter.

Several descendants of bear leaders from Ariège immigrated to the United States and some to Canada; some of them opened restaurants in the 1950s. We could therefore taste typical Ariège dishes in Manhattan restaurants such as Les Pyrénées, La Pergola des Artistes and Le Rivage.

The last two still in activity are managed by Christian PONSOLLE for one and Paul DENAMIEL for the other. At La Pergola des artistes, photographs of bear performers decorate the walls.

In New York City there still remain vestiges of the time of the bear performers. Formerly, every Sunday afternoon in good weather, bear performers and their compatriots met at a place in Central Park called Sheep Meadow. They gathered there around a rock which took the name of Roc d'Ercé. Their descendants still go there occasionally.

Photographs and Images

A picture is worth a thousand words. Several photographs and drawings witness to the bear performers' visit to Quebec and eastern Canada, the United States, France, England and Scotland. The first photographs date from 1890, the last from the 1900s.

Looking at these images is like making a voyage in the industry of the Ariège bear leader that is the farmer become showman.

The costume evolved very little in those years except for the hat, the original beret gave way to the hat of the country visited. The ritual of showing the bear—imitating the shepherd, making the damsel, sitting on a stool—has also evolved very little. Some additions were made to please North Americans like having the bear climb a tree and wear a small hat.

When the bear performer joined a circus, then the showman's costume changed and so did the show. The fight between two bears was also popular, and the costume of their trainer became less folkloric.

Roc d'Ercé, Sheep Meadow, Central Park, New York.

Source: Marie-Joëlle Parent, April 2014.

Methodology

Research on the life of bear performers requires crosschecking several data from different sources on given individuals. The data on these migrants are scattered in several archival banks in Ariège, England, the United States and Quebec and are difficult to collect.

Ariège...

Two trips to Ariège in 2010 and 2013 made it possible for the author to understand the family structures of the Ariégeois and, moreover, the consultation of the archives contained in the Civil Registers of the French State for births, marriages and deaths accessible in the town halls deepened this understanding. These trips became also an opportunity to collect testimonials from local descendants of bear performers as well as some family albums photographs. In addition, if an Ariégeois had died abroad, the mayor then was annotating in the margins of the birth certificate of that person his date and place of death, a mention which in many cases has facilitated the identification.

The archives related to the military life of the Ariégeois were of great help, because they contain notes relating to the movements abroad and the consular registers in the countries visited by the travelers. Moreover, when a young man was declared "Absent" following an order to report to the army and was later declared "Insoumis" meaning rebellious, there was a good chance that this person had left the country, often with a bear to make his living. The archives of those "Morts pour la France" (i.e. Dead while battling for the motherland) and of those wounded during the 1914–1918 war gave precious indications on the migrating routes of the Ariégeois.

The archives of the life of the bear performers, especially, the registers of bear performer notebooks granted in the French town halls, are particularly useful. The declarations of departure to the local police are also useful and are recorded in the military registers.

Britain...

The bear performers who came to Quebec were only passing through Britain, but by showing the bear on the way, they left traces. Photographs found in several towns such as Arundel, Glasgow, Ipswich, London, Morley, Norfolk, North Lancashire, Oxfordshire, Ruardean, Sedgley and Westgate, and newspaper articles are precious testimonies of their passage. In these pieces, one can read reports on the tricks of the bear used for entertaining crowds who only rarely saw bears which had been previously eradicated in England, and sometimes about misbehavior like crowding public roads or animal abuse (rare).

Some bear performers even appeared in the English census which can therefore be another source to crosscheck when they came and where the bear handlers went prior embarking for North America.

Finally, the lists of passengers departing Liverpool from 1900 onwards helped to compare the names with the arrival lists at the ports of Quebec and Montreal.

The United States...

Some 200 Ariège bear performers traveled to and through the United States between 1871 and 1914. They left several traces in newspapers, censuses, applications for naturalization, and passenger lists. Visiting the Castle Garden and Ellis Island archives was more than helpful in following the bear performers' routes.

An absolute record for the number of Ariège bear leaders was set when the steamship SS CHATEAU LEOVILLE arrived at the port of New York on March 22, 1883, with fourteen bear performers from Oust and Ercé. They had sailed from Bordeaux; those coming directly to Quebec sailed from Liverpool or Glasgow.

The Ports of Québec City and Montreal

The 93 bear performers who came to Quebec were first traced by arrivals at the ports of Québec City and Montreal. Manifest information was used to identify them. This information is written in English. In this book, bear performers who came to Quebec are listed by order of arrival of the ships. Here the record number of bear performers arriving on the same ship is eight, as you will find in the following pages.

The data relating to the movements of these men in Quebec were found in the registers to the Consulates of Québec City and Montreal, in the Canadian censuses from 1891 to 1921. A few newspaper articles and a few rare photographs on the territory gave directions to follow the itinerary of their nomadic lives.

In general, to carry out this kind of research, especially in the archives classified by keyword, it is not necessary to limit oneself to the only term of "montreur d'ours" that is rarely used in Quebec and elsewhere. Thus, in the six years of research commissioned by this book, a lexicon of words and terms used in archives and literature has developed. Any of these terms can be found in the passenger manifests or in the archives.

In Occitan: Orsalher;

In French: Oussaillé, Montreur d'ours, Ours dansant, Dresseur d'ours, Conducteur d'animaux et Saltimbanque ;

In English: Bear Handler, Bear Leader, Bear Tamer, Bear Trainer, Bear Keeper, Bear Performer, Circus, Bear, Conductor of Animals, Dancing Bear, Frenchman with Bears, Performer, Performing Bear, Showman, Tame Bear, Tamer, Touring Bear Performer and Trick Bear;

and in Italian: Orsanti.

Travelers coming down to the ports of Québec City or Montreal had impressive views of the St. Lawrence River and of prominent buildings on its shore. Customs and reception buildings were reserved for passengers; they were greeted in English.

Except where specially mentioned in the text, the statements contained therein come from the military registers of the Ariège, that is from "Carnets de saltimbanques" (busker's notebook) issued by the departmental authorities, and civil status documents. To lighten the text, we will not refer to these archives specifically. Only references differing from these usual sources will be mentioned.

Chapter 2

The 1870s: Seniors' reconnaissance trips

The 1870s were significant in the history of bear performers in America and especially in Quebec. The first arrival in New York is in the fall of 1871, from Glasgow, of Alexis AURIAC Roc, Bernard ROGALLE Clar and Guillaume FAUR Jouanillou.

The first arrival in Quebec is three years later, in the fall of 1874. It was not until 1877 that other bear performers arrived. In all, six bear performers roamed the soil of Quebec in the 1870s. Meanwhile, arrivals at New York, Philadelphia and New Orleans multiplied: sixteen ships carrying twenty-one Pyrenean bear leaders have been indexed.

1874-09-06 SS PERUVIAN from Liverpool to Québec City

Two passengers bearing Ariégeois names, Jean BROUÉ, ticket number 2452 and Pierre BACQUÉ, ticket number 2456, went ashore in September at the port of Québec City.

Biography of Jean BROUÉ Samsou

Born on October 26, 1843, in Arrous, Jean is the uncle of my direct ancestor Jean BROUÉ Cabillot. He has the distinction of being the first BROUÉ native of Oust to obtain in 1867 a "Carnet de saltimbanque" (Busker's notebook) as a bear performer. In addition, he is the first to land in Quebec with a dancing bear. It is interesting to ponder what drives an unmarried man to cross France along the railroad to Le Havre, take a small boat to Southampton and from there to Liverpool in order to show the bear and collect coins in his big beret.

Jean BROUÉ Samsou being the tenth child of his family, his economic future looked rather bleak. The paternal land being passed on to the oldest son, the other boys must either find a wife who owns land or "upstream", that is to say, clear land in hamlets in the high mountains; girls, on the other hand, must find a husband who owns land with a rather thin dowry to offer when coming from a big family. The trade of bear tamer, especially for those who came to America, permitted to raise enough money for the establishment of a young family.

Jean BROUÉ began his career as a bear performer at 24 years of age by obtaining a "Carnet de saltimbanque" in 1867 with his brother Pierre, and the following year he obtained a second "carnet" with three other bear performers. After a first trip to America, he married in 1877 Joséphine GÉRAUD Binsou in Oust, twelve years his junior. The children were born between 1878 and 1895. His two boys, Jean, born in 1881, a bear leader, and Joseph, born in 1895, died in France during the 1914–1918 war. He undertook other campaigns, including one in the United States in 1882 with his brother Joseph and four other compatriots as evidenced on first-hand, by notarized papers dated 1879, 1882, 1885 and 1896 concerning the management of his property in his absence and, on the other hand, by the listed boat crossings, one between Bordeaux and New York and one to Quebec.

An excerpt from a notarial contract of 1885 clearly mentions his profession:

«Jean GÉRAUD Grill from Arrous declares having received from Jean BROUÉ SAMSOU d'Arrous, absent, but represented by Josephine GÉRAUD (Binsou) his wife accepting for her husband, at the moment in the Americas as a bear driver. » 1885-12-06, notary act of Me GÉRAUD, Oust. (translation by the author)

In 1899 he appeared again at the Port of Québec City, accompanied by four compatriots and two bears.

After this last trip in 1899, he sold his land in Arrous and moved with his daughters to Couthures-sur-Garonne. In the census of 1906, he lives with one of his daughters and his son-in-law. He is not mentioned in the census of 1911. As for Josephine GÉRAUD Binsou, she had died in 1906.

Jean BROUÉ and his two brothers Joseph and Pierre were professional bear performers and pioneers of the trade.

1877-06-28 SS SARMATIAN from Liverpool to Québec City

Four Ercé bear performers sharing ticket number 1606 landed at the Port of Québec City.

We can decipher the names of Pierre SERVAT, Jean SERVAT, P. RIVIERE and Jean BÉNAZET. To identify them, it was necessary to consult the military registers and the SERVAT family archives.

Chapter 3

The 1880s: the birth of the dancing bear
industry in North America

In the 1880s, the dancing bear industry was booming in America. Ten ships brought some thirty performers and their dancing bears to the ports of Montreal and Québec City. These men and a woman departed mainly in the spring from Liverpool, with the exception of two from Glasgow and one from Belfast, and arrived in Quebec in the months of May, June and July.

The 1870s were years of exploration, the showmen returned to Ariège and according to their testimonies, an ideal and profitable itinerary begins to take shape. Ideal because safe for bears and men and profitable for those men who did leave penniless.

1880-05-03 SS LAKE WINNIPEG from Liverpool to Québec City

Two men left Liverpool on the Lake Winnipeg on April 15, 1880, and arrived in Quebec only on May 3, eighteen days of crossing with their bears. Jean Mathielas PEYRAT and Jean Pierre ESPERTE are entered in the passengers' list as Conductors of Animals.

1881-05-12 SS LAKE CHAMPLAIN from Liverpool to Québec City

On ticket number 432, four men designate themselves as Showmen.

On the manifest of the LAKE CHAMPLAIN, the names of CUGOL Joseph, Baptiste MAURY, GÉRAUD André and CAUJOLLE Jean, all in their twenties, can be deciphered.

The names are difficult to read and to identify, but an article in the Manchester Evening News chronicles had mentioned the arrest by police of Frenchmen with bears in early April, just before their departure from Liverpool.

Passers-by reported to the police that bear showmen were regularly beating the animal. What passers-by did not understand was that some light tapping was needed to move the trained bear. Two of the men were fined, and the two others were imprisoned for a few days. This "brutality" is unusual for the Pyrenean showmen because their bears were their livelihood and there was always a risk that the bear would take revenge. Even trained, the brown bear remained an animal with unpredictable behavior.

Biography of André GÉRAUD Parracha

Born on August 16, 1850, in Arrous, he was the greatest traditional bear showman in Quebec. He always showed the bear in the Pyrenean tradition and never joined an American circus. His career was prolific and, above all, punctuated by numerous trips to France, England and North America.

After his military service in 1874, André obtained a booklet allowing him limited stays inside France. He thus visited with his bear a very vast territory: Hautes-Alpes, Corrèze, la Vienne, Montreuil Largillé (Eure), Moulins La Marche (Orne), Montdoubleau (Loir-et-Cher) and Sancoins. He traveled several hundred kilometres in four years.

On March 2, 1878, by then in America, he was declared "Rebellious" by the French army and sentenced to fifteen days in prison for neglecting to validate his military log at the consulate.

When he returned, he signed a marriage contract, written by Me GÉRAUD in Oust, with Anne ANDREU d'Alios from the neighboring hamlet. They were married two years later in 1880 and settled in Miramont, a hamlet of Oust. They had three children: Jean, Jeanne and Joseph. The oldest Jean, bear performer, had a tragic fate in 1916 in the famous battle of Verdun, killed by enemy fire.

In 1880, he took the road again with his bear and visited several towns and villages, including Saint James (Manche), Doué La Fontaine (Maine and Loire) and Nontron (Dordogne) after stopping at Villefranche de Belves, Puy Levêque, Fumel, Montcucq and Lauzerte. More kilometres…

After a brief stay at home, he left for a new journey. We find his trace in England in early April 1881, where he went to court with his three companions for mistreating a bear. The judge ordered him to pay a fine of five schillings or to remain in prison for five to seven days. He chooses to pay the deposit, as did one of his friends; the other two remained in prison. Finally, out of trouble, they all four embarked at Liverpool for Québec City. They will not linger in the city and will continue their journey to Montreal and ultimately New York. A year later, he boarded back in New York for France.

André GÉRAUD Parracha returned to England in the spring of 1884, returned to the fold in August 1884, and in June 1885, the choppy life will resume. He arrived in Canada with Jean BROUÉ Cabillot, a nineteen-year-old man and another compatriot. Two events will occur during his absence: the death of his father Guillaume, and the birth of his daughter Marie Anne in July 1885.

In March 1886, a notarial act signed by proxy by his brother Jean Paul attested to his presence in America. Here is an excerpt:

"Jean GÉRAUD Gril acknowledges and declares to have received from Sieur André GÉRAUD Parracha, of Arrous, absent at this moment and traveling in America as a bear driver, but represented by his brother Jean Paul GÉRAUD." Me Vidal, Oust, March 3, 1886. (translation by the author)

In 1887, also in America, he made the news in Monroeville, Kentucky. According to the Fort Wayne Daily Gazette of October 11, 1887, some drunken men killed his bear. These men were sentenced, but they appealed and we do not know the outcome of the story. Deprived of his livelihood, André GÉRAUD returned home after three years of absence.

After acquiring another bear, he again took up the trade and, unlike his habit of leaving from Liverpool, he went to the port of Bordeaux. He landed in New York on May 28, 1889, with his brothers, Guillaume and Jean Pierre, and six other compatriots. They all declared to go to Montreal.

In 1889 he lodged in Chaboillez Square in Montreal, and in 1890 he reported to the Montreal Consulate.

After a short stay back in Arrous, he left again in 1891 for Liverpool and Montreal. On September 2, 1891, he declared that he wanted to settle in Montreal by registering at the Consulate.

In 1892 and 1894 he showed the bear in New York State with his brother Jean Pierre.

On May 29, 1899, he arrived in Québec City on SS Ruapehu accompanied by his brother Jean Pierre, Jean BROUÉ Samsou, Baptiste HUGHET Lagusat and Pierre ROGALLE Luciat Gudanes. After a two-year stay, in December 1901, he sailed from Montreal to Liverpool on the SS Vancouver.

He came back later between 1902 and 1905 again with his brother Jean Pierre, and then returned home on October 28, 1905, on the SS Tunisian from Quebec to Liverpool. There were five bear performers making this trip back to Europe.

In 1907, he left again Liverpool on the ship Welshman for Portland, Maine and Montreal. He was accompanied by Jean Pierre his brother, and Pierre SPERTE a compatriot. He made a long stay in Montreal at the DURRACQ Hotel located on 3162 Notre-Dame Street West. His brother joined him in February 1909.

In 1910, at the age of sixty, he stopped altogether his travels. He had earned enough money to buy land in Arrous and ensure the well-being of his family. Unfortunately, two of his children have died in the years that followed: his daughter Marie Anne "died in childbirth" and his son Jean died at the Battle of Verdun. His son Joseph became the only heir to the family patrimony generated by all these trips with the bear.

André GÉRAUD Parracha died a few years later in 1919 on his land in Oust, and his wife died in 1933. Parracha will remain etched in the

Ariège collective memory as one of the greatest bear showmen and certainly one of the most enthusiastic of Quebec.

1881-06-07 SS LAKE NEPIGON from Liverpool to Québec City

Four bear performers show up on ticket 1370. One of them had an eventful life…

Biography of Bernard ROGALLE Clar

Born on July 9, 1830, in Cominac, he was granted a life surrounded by bear tamers, a life well filled, though difficult. His three nephews Bernard, Jean and Jean-Pierre ROGALLE Clar Jacolle Petiou were great bear showmen in Quebec in the 1900s.

In 1855, Bernard participated in the Crimean War and his life changed… He lost his left arm during a battle. He was awarded the Military Medal of the Crimean War. Working the land in Cominac was no longer an option, he rather opted to practice the job of bear handler full time. He was the pioneer of the industry in 1871 and immigrated to Canada. He died in Montreal in 1889 and is buried in the Notre-Dame-des-Neiges Cemetery.

His great-granddaughter Françoise LEWIS is living today in Montreal and she is still carrying out extensive research on her ancestors, their lives and their trades.

***

"—Wednesday bear tamers arrived in this city with three of these ferocious animals. They made them act a pantomime and perform many skilled tricks. It was fun." Le Messager of Nicolet, 1881.

1885-06-18 SS BROOKLYN from Liverpool to Montreal

On ticket 677, there are three foreigners going to Montreal. One of the names is not clear and the other two are known bear performers. One of them, Jean BROUÉ Cabillot, is the ancestor of the author of this book.

Biography of Jean BROUÉ Cabillot

Born September 28, 1865, in Arrous, he was only nineteen years old when he arrived in Montreal in 1885 from Liverpool with his two fellow showmen. His uncle Joseph BROUÉ Samsou with whom he showed the bear in England, followed him a few weeks later.

Before boarding the boat at Liverpool on June 4, 1885, the young man had become known in England. In fact, an article in The Illustrated Police News of June 1885, A Performing Bear in Court, related the passage in the West-Ham Court near London of two BROUÉ, an old man and a young man, accompanied by a bear. They were released on bail and the formal promise to no longer disturb public order.

Broué Sr. referred to in the article is Joseph BROUÉ Samsou, the uncle of my grandfather Jean BROUÉ Cabillot. The young man of nineteen years called Jacques BROUÉ in the article is none other than Jean BROUÉ Cabillot Two facts establish this: Jean BROUÉ Cabillot is declared "Absent with Leave" at the roll call of the class 1885 of the French army, he therefore had left Ariège before reaching his twentieth year. Moreover, there is no BROUÉ whose first name is Jacques in the BROUÉ Ariégeois clan, which leads us to believe that most likely the policeman and the journalist misunderstood the given name of Jean with Occitan accent.

Jean BROUÉ the Ariégeois

Jean BROUÉ, well established in Ariège was the son of Pierre BROUÉ Cabillot of Ustou and Marianne CAU Ramoun known as Cabillot d'Ercé.

A farmer on the land of his parents until his departure, Jean BROUÉ was well integrated into the social fabric of the hamlet. He left Ariège and his family after a disagreement with his father about the military service of three years at the time. His military record of Ariège showed that he was called up just before his departure for America and thereafter, he is declared "Absent with Leave" and finally "Away without Leave" for not having returned to the country to serve his three years in the army.

Jean BROUÉ in Saint-André-Avellin

Between 1885 and 1890, Jean showed the bear in Canada and the United States. In July 1890 he bought land from the former seigneury of the Petite-Nation in western Quebec, 136 kilometres from Montreal, which belonged to the family of Louis-Joseph Papineau and where his friend Jean RIEU Casteilla was already living. This trip to America was crucial for him, he met then a young French-Canadian girl named Philomène GAUTHIER whom in 1890 he got married with in the village of Saint-André-Avellin. From this pioneer couple are descended all the BROUÉ families in Quebec and the BROUE families in the state of New York.

Marriage of Jean BROUÉ Cabillot and Philomène GAUTHIER in Saint-André-Avellin in 1890.

They had seven children: Émile in 1892, Marie-Laure in 1893, Jean-Baptiste and his stillborn twin in 1895, Ariste in 1898, Adélard in 1901 and Béatrice in 1902. Unfortunately four of them died at an early age but the other three did overcome adversity and led a well-filled life. They are Jean-Baptiste, Ariste and Beatrice.

As the Canadian censuses of 1891 and 1901 show, the family peacefully lived and farmed the land in Saint-André-Avellin. Jean BROUÉ became a Canadian citizen in 1904. In the meantime, he still made occasional trips to show the bear, along with his friend Alfred ROGALLE Péou d'Arrous arrived in Quebec in 1903 via New York.

Exile in the United States

In 1909, the family exiled itself in the United States. On the list of CANADA-US border crossings for July 1909, the complete family is named BROE: John Broe, Philomen, Harris, John Baptist and Beatrice. It's a lot like our family in Saint-André-Avellin. BROE, it's BROUE; John, it's Jean the father; Philomen is Philomène the mother; Harris is American-style Ariste; John Baptist is Jean-Baptiste and Beatrice is Béatrice. They applied for entry in the United States at the St-Armand Crossing Point—Rouses Point, a land border on Lake Champlain slightly southeast of the village of Lacolle in Quebec.

It is stated in this document that their final destination is Glens Falls in the state of New York. Following the list of family members, we find the name of Peter MAURY who is also traveling to Glens Falls. Mention is made that he gave as reference the name of his cousin Maurice Dorac whose address is 1363 Notre Dame St, Montreal. It's quite obvious he is in fact Pey MAURY Bourriquet born in 1864 in Ercé. Pey is Pierre in Occitan. The cousin is Maurice DURRACQ, the owner of the Commercial Hotel on Notre-Dame Street in Montreal.

What were they doing in Glens Falls? The answer is given by the US census of 1910. The small BREWIS family: John, Philene, John, Ira and Beatrice appear in full. It is undeniably the BROUÉ family, Jean, 45, Philomène 36 and the three living children, Jean-Baptiste 14, Harris [Ariste], 12, and Beatrice, 7. They are identified as French-Canadian immigrants to the United States, but not naturalized. There is no trace of Pierre MAURY who had crossed the border with them in 1909.

This 1910 census document is very interesting. It says the whole family speaks English except the father and the youngest child. Jean does not read and write English but the others do, except the youngest. Astonishing for a globetrotter! The older children go to school.

The head of the family was hired by Cement Works of Glens Falls as a quarryman. It is indicated in the census that Jean BROUÉ did not miss work during the previous year having become a foreman. In this "Company town" (small town built by a company especially for its workers), the BROUÉs are housed at Glens Falls Ward 1, unit number 173. This seems to be a small house according to plans. It should be noted that the numbers were changed in 1946-47, well after their departure.

Tuberculosis changes the destiny of the family

Around 1911, Jean-Baptiste BROUÉ, their eldest son, sixteen years old at the time, became ill with tuberculosis and was sent to Quebec to the family of his mother Philomène for care. The fresh air of the Laurentians had a good reputation. He has never returned to the United States to live. When his parents Jean BROUÉ and Philomène GAUTHIER themselves returned to Quebec in 1920, the two other children, Harris, then twenty-one, and Béatrice, seventeen, remained in the United States and became American citizens. Jean BROUÉ and Philomène GAUTHIER have settled in Quebec in 1920, in time to attend the baptism of my mother Madeleine BROUÉ, born July 22, 1920, daughter of Jean-Baptiste BROUÉ and Berthe LATOUR. The godfather, Jean BROUÉ and the godmother, Philomène GAUTHIER, signed the baptismal certificate on July 24, 1920.

On his return to Quebec, Jean BROUÉ Cabillot began the last part of his career. He bought a farm in Longue-Pointe, Montreal, on Lepailleur Street near the harbor and he worked at Dominion Park, an amusement park on the St. Lawrence River, taking care of the bears, of course.

Jean BROUÉ Cabillot and Philomène GAUTHIER in Longue-Pointe, Montreal in 1920.

He died on December 25, 1932, at the age of sixty-seven, and was buried in Montreal East Cemetery while his wife, Philomène, died in 1936, having for a few years interestingly enough rubbed shoulders with Alfred ROGALLE Péou, the old friend of the family.

What happened to his Ariège family?

It is remarkable to note that Jean's parents Pierre BROUÉ and Marianne CAU came to Quebec in 1890 for the marriage of their son. They had liquidated all their possessions in Arrous shortly after their departure. Had they planned to immigrate to Quebec? They are in the census of 1891 in Saint-André-Avellin and later we are finding them in Layrac in the Lot-et-Garonne where they had been living out with their daughter Marie, their other child. The climate of Quebec and the harsh life of the settlers probably decided them to return to France to live with their daughter. They will again see their son Jean, who meanwhile became a Canadian citizen, only in 1913 when he returned to visit his dying mother. As he had previously obtained an amnesty from the French army, he was able to go to France without risking imprisonment. He got this pardon because of his age, approaching fifty. Marie, his only sister, married Jean PUJOL Andréou d'Escampis, Oust, and died in 1925 in Layrac. She had four children, including Léon PUJOL who "died for France" in 1918.

What happened to his descendants in America?

Jean-Baptiste BROUÉ is at the origin of the BROUÉ family branch living in Quebec…

Jean-Baptiste BROUÉ married Berthe LATOUR in Montreal in 1919. They had eleven children. Ten of these eleven children survived and founded families. They, in turn, had a flock of children. There are now six generations of BROUÉ Cabillot in Quebec, about ninety people. As of 2015, the surname BROUÉ is still carried by twenty-eight of them.

Harris and Beatrice became the BROUEs of New York State…

Harris BROUE's family…

Harris BROUE, whose original name Ariste was definitely abandoned in favor of the American version, married Loretta E. DUNN in the United States. They had two children: Rose and Harry Jr. They lived in Troy and ran a restaurant called The Mansion in Albany, New York. They came to Montreal several times in the 1940s and 1960s.

Their daughter Rose BROUE married Joseph WHITMAN. They had two daughters in the years 1945-50: Marlene WHITMAN became Mrs. Edward ECKHARDT and Shirley WHITMAN became Mrs. Worthington PARKER. Did these two couples have children?

Harry BROUE married Theresa ROBINSON in England at the end of World War II. The couple settled in Troy. Two children were born of their union: Melanie Elisabeth and Mitchell Paul. Did they get married, did they have children? Sadly, Melanie Elizabeth died of cancer in 2003 at the age of fifty-three. Mitchell Paul BROUE born in 1954 would be the only American with the original surname BROUE Cabillot unless he has children.

Beatrice BROUÉ's family…

Beatrice BROUÉ got married very young to Nicolas EISELEIN, an English immigrant from New York. From this union were born Louise, Robert and

Wallace, the EISELEIN family lived for a time in Quebec in the 1920s and their members became thereafter entirely American. Beatrice then remarried in the 1940s to Albert STRUMLAUF, an Austrian immigrant of Jewish religion. His children kept the surname EISELEIN, which they officially transformed into ESLYN during the 1939-45 war.

Louise, the eldest of the children, became Mrs. ROSELLO. My mother, Madeleine BROUÉ in her youth, was very close to her cousin she called Loulou. She had five children who all live in Long Island, New York.

Robert, the second, was married to a woman named Helen and lived in North Carolina with their three children. Wallace, the youngest, married Nola and they had five children. Wallace ESLYN had a distinguished career in forestry and lived with his family in Wisconsin.

All this information on the New York State BROUE was obtained through consultation of newspapers and various archives. I have only been in contact with the descendants since very recently. The last direct contact was a phone call from cousin Loulou during the Montreal World Fair in 1967. After passing on family news, she asked if French was still spoken in Montreal. This gives an idea of the cultural gap between the two branches of BROUÉ forming the descendants of Ariégeois Jean BROUÉ Cabillot, one completely Americanized speaking English only and the other Québécois speaking French.

1885-07-02 SS TORONTO from Liverpool to Montreal

Joseph BROUÉ, Pierre BÉNAZET and the two CAUJOLLE brothers appeared on the same ticket, number 1369.

Biography of Joseph BROUÉ Samsou.

Born on March 4, 1839, in Arrous, he is the seventh child of Jean Pierre BROUÉ Samsou and Marguerite GÉRAUD Parracha. He is the uncle of Jean BROUÉ Cabillot, the young man who arrived on the previous ship. He married Catherine GÉRAUD Laurent de Paule in Oust in 1868. They had four children between 1868 and 1877, two boys and two girls. The two boys Jean Pierre and Jean became bear performers like their father.

Joseph first came to America in March 1882 with his brother Jean, who had pioneered bear performing in Quebec in 1874. They arrived in New York on the CHATEAU LEOVILLE from Liverpool. Other compatriots accompany them, SIRGANT, GÉRAUD and Vincent ROZÈS Barlabé, a bear showman.

His second trip will be on the TORONTO from Liverpool to Montreal.

Before boarding in Liverpool, while he was showing the bear with his nephew Jean BROUÉ Cabillot, he was arrested at West Ham in the eastern suburbs of London. He is the BROUÉ of fifty-two years who is named in the article "A Performing Bear in court." After this adventure, he entrusted his young nephew Jean BROUÉ to André GÉRAUD Parracha. They arrived in Montreal on June 18, 1885, in Montreal. Two weeks later, July 2, 1885, Joseph BROUÉ Samsou, Jacques Pierre BÉNAZET and the two CAUJOLLE brothers followed. Joseph is forty-seven years old, and this will be his last big trip to the bear.

On May 18, 1890, his cousin Pierre BROUÉ Cabillot gave him power of attorney for the management of the school in the hamlet of Arrous and in 1891, he signed the lease. He took possession of the house that lodged the school and took care of it until his death on February 13, 1907. This house still exists in Arrous.

His sons Jean Pierre and Jean continued the tradition of showing the bear as evidenced by a notarized contract on September 12, 1897, in which Joseph signed "for his sons Jean-Pierre and Jean who are in America acting as bear drivers". They had a long stay which lasted seven years.

In the fall of 1885, news came out that the SS Brooklyn, the ship which the bear performers had boarded in June to make the crossing, was shipwrecked (The Montreal Daily Witness, Nov. 11, 1885).

The SS Brooklyn of the Dominion Line is the ship boarded by Jean BROUÉ Cabillot in June 1885. This ship had faced adversity many times and accidents had been reported, but this time the shock was fatal, the ship ran ashore on Anticosti Island in the middle of the St. Lawrence River. The crew spent the winter on the island while waiting for help. There were no deaths.

In addition to the sinking, another event affected the life of the adventurers in 1885 and changed their route.

The seven bear performers who arrived in Montreal in 1885 were not aware that at the same time, the population of Montreal was undergoing a serious smallpox epidemic that was going to claim more than 3000 lives. This epidemic greatly contributed to the exodus of the showmen that year. They migrated south through Vermont to presumably spend the winter in New York City where they could work in hotels while the animals slept quietly at the Central Park Zoo or in a barn not far away.

1886-05-17 SS MONTREAL from Belfast to Québec City

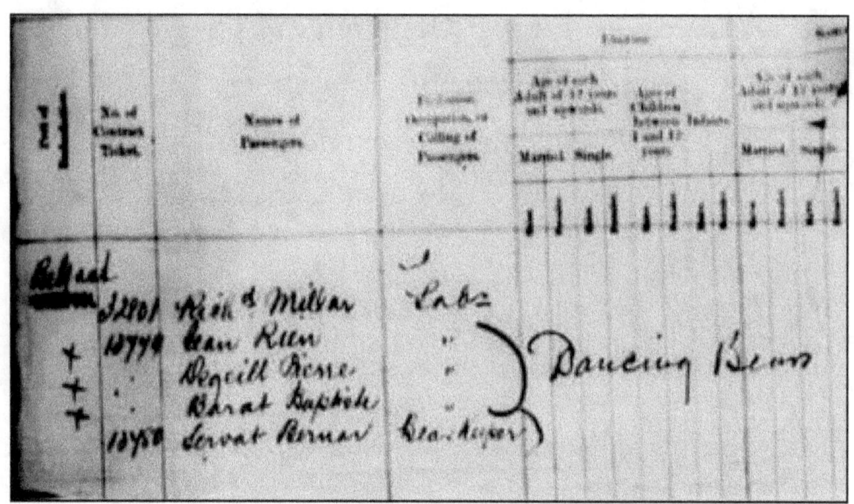

List of passengers of the SS MONTREAL. Three Laborers with Dancing Bears and a Bear Keeper.

Four Ariégeois and three bears got on this ship leaving Belfast for Quebec. Three bear performers: Jean RIEU, Pierre DÉGEILH, Baptiste BARAT appeared on ticket # 12,779 with three dancing bears and a bear trainer, Bernard SERVAT, accompanied them with ticket #12,780.

***

"Beasts in Court" and "Ban on Bears Dancing" are titles found in Montreal newspapers in 1886.

1887-06-02 SS GRECIAN from Glasgow to Québec City

The inscription on the manifest of "Six Frenchmen with bears for Quebec" leaves no doubt about the trades practiced by these

Frenchmen—numbers 2 to 7—departing from Glasgow. Few performers traveled that far north to take a ship to North America. These bear performers would have seen an opportunity to increase their nest egg and the opportunity to improve their English before leaving for America.

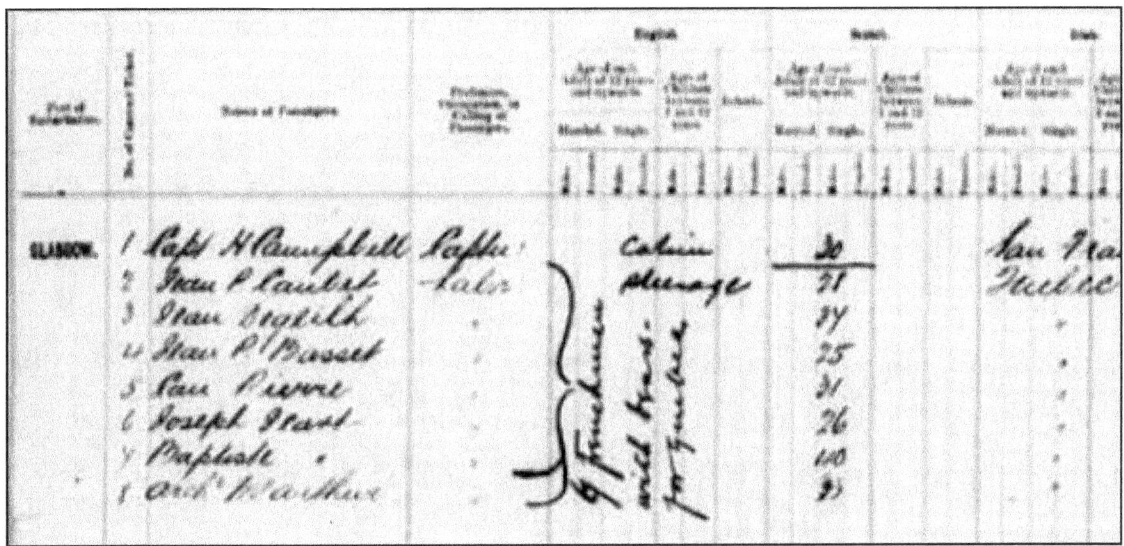

Frenchman with Bears for Quebec, excerpt from SS GRECIAN's manifest from Glasgow to Quebec.

Biography of Jean DÉGEILH Courate

Born on August 23, 1862, in Cominac, Jean followed in the footsteps of his brother Pierre who came to Quebec in 1886. He was exempted from military service for three years because he had a brother already serving. In January 1887, carrying a "Carnet de saltimbanque" (Busker's notebook), he set out with compatriots and went to Glasgow. He returned home in October 1890 and later we come across him again in March 1893 when he landed in New York, alone, traveling from Le Havre.

He then met other bear performers, and together they traveled all along the east coast of the United States. In August 1895, things got complicated for him and took a dramatic turn, as reported in the New York Times in 1895.

"Killed One Man, Wounded Two. Farmer McComb, of Summitville, Fires Buckshot into a Group of Five Frenchmen, They had Trick Bears." Wednesday, August 14, 1895. New York Herald, page 12.

The names are identified in the article: Jean DEGEILH Courate, Jean HUGUET Balent, Lucien ITTÉ, Guillaume Jean LAUREAUX and Jean Pierre ANDREU.

Jean DEGEILH Courate was the man killed by farmer McComb in Summitville. This sad news was communicated to the mayor of Ercé by the companions who returned to France following this tragic event. The French army was not informed of the death of Jean, he was even declared "Away Without Leave" in 1896.

1889-07-23 SS SIBERIAN from Glasgow to Québec City

Some Ariégeois on this ship, at numbers 42 and 43, Jean SOUQUET and Jean ICART who each call themselves "Showman" and at numbers 48 and 49, Joseph and Jean AJAS, two farmers who obtained land in Western Canada. The two bear performers led full lives as it can be evidenced by their experiences.

Biography of Jean SOUQUET Malet

Born on October 28, 1861, in Escalusse, hamlet of Ercé, he traveled a lot and also tried his hand at entrepreneurship. Being a bear performer and provided with a "Carnet de saltimbanque" at seventeen, he gave shows in France before doing his military service from 1883 to 1886 in Tunisia. In 1889, he decided to cross to America with Jean ICART Moumat, traveling first to England and Scotland, then to Canada. After a two-year stay in North America, in January 1892 he embarked in Honolulu for Australia with his bear. He founded a small circus and announced in the newspapers under the name: "The Souquet Brothers Champion Animal Trainers." He performed under this name for some time in Australia and New Zealand, giving performances to people who had never seen a bear. Success was immediate.

Jean SOUQUET made a short stay at Ercé in 1893 and returned the following year to New Zealand with three compatriots from France: Raymond PONSOLLE Laouzé, Jean ROGALLE Labat and his sister Anna ROGALLE Labat. The circus "The Souquet Brothers" now had three bear performers and an assistant Anna who traveled across Australia and New Zealand.

When the business began to decline, Jean SOUQUET sold his circus and his animals and joined the "Wirth Brothers" circus for a few years. Anna, by then his wife, and their two sons went with him.

It was finally at Mount Cargill in New Zealand that he settled permanently, acquiring citizenship in 1910. Until his death on April 17, 1928, he was a farmer with the help of his seven boys and three girls, all New Zealanders. Anna survived him until 1950.

1889-10-14 SS SARDINIAN from Liverpool to Montreal

On ticket number 1643, there are three women this time: Maria RAYMOND, Maria ROGALLE and Marie ROGALLE, her sister. Their father Bernard ROGALLE Clar, having died in Montreal in September 1889, the two ROGALLE sisters went to Montreal to take care of his business. Mrs. RAYMOND from Montreal accompanied them and then gave them work in Montreal. The three women made a very long trip from the Pyrenees to Liverpool before embarking for Montreal.

Chapter 4

The 1890s:the showmen and their bears conquer North America

1890 was a record year for arrivals of Ariège bear showmen in Quebec. The oldest of the villages having demonstrated that it is possible to earn a lot of money while crossing in America, their sons or their nephews tried their hand at the adventure.

Between April 11 and September 9 of that year, four ships docked at the ports of Quebec, disembarking twenty-one bear performers. The first ship of the year arrived in Montreal in late April from Liverpool and had on board eight bear performers, a record!

The number of bears is not always specified on the passenger lists, but it may be supposed that in the spring and summer of 1890, eight to ten bears performed their tours directed by their masters on the roads of Quebec and the United States.

The years from 1891 to 1899 were quieter. Eight ships docked at Quebec or Montreal, disembarking twenty-one bear performers. A typical and well-honed itinerary emerges—Departure from Ariège in February or March, England for a few months, the port of Liverpool and boarding around May or June for Quebec or Montreal.

1890-04-30 SS LAKE NEPIGON from Liverpool to Montreal

The bear performers who traveled on this ship could be sorted out through the passengers' lists of those ships departing from Liverpool on April 11, 1890. Eight Ariégeois on ticket number 2196 are among the thirty-six passengers leaving on SS LAKE NEPIGON that day.

The passengers' manifest of LAKE NEPIGON on arrival in Montreal is nowhere to be found, but since this vessel opened the 1890 navigation season at the Port of Montreal, it is mentioned in the Navy Department's Annual Report presented to the Parliament of Ottawa. We can then confirm the arrival of the Ariégeois. Two other ships, OREGON and SARDINIAN arrived the same day, but they left six days later than LAKE NEPIGON, while still attempting to arrive first at the Port of Montreal.

The voyage started by SS LAKE NEPIGON on April 11th proved to be long and perilous, the eight bear performers on board had to fear for their lives and that of their bears.

According to the New York Herald of May 2, 1890 (page 10), the steamship was ice-trapped in Cape Ray, Newfoundland for six days. The ice having finally moved from under the ship, it continued its course not without risk to capsize. Thirty-six passengers almost panicked when the ship was again caught in ice on April 22. This time, the SS SAMSON helped free the ship.

On April 30, then, safe and sound, the eighth bear performers sharing ticket number 2196 disembarked at the Port of Montreal.

1890-05-22 SS SIBERIAN from Glasgow to Québec City

On May 22, 1890, the citizens of Lévis saw arriving, after thirteen days at sea, strange travelers: six men and four trained bears.

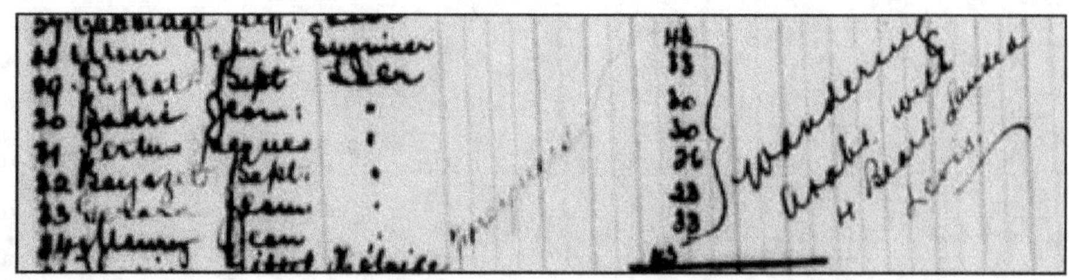

Manifest of arrival of SS SIBERIAN states the following on May 22, 1890:

"Foreigners, Wandering Arabs with 4 Bears Landed Lévis"

Indeed, under numbers 29 to 34, six foreigners between the ages of twenty-three and thirty-three who were described as itinerant Arabs with four bears did land in Lévis on opposite shore of Québec City. Departing from the Pyrenees in early February, they went to Glasgow, Scotland and from there, on May 9, boarded the SIBERIAN for Quebec. On arrival in Lévis, they had been mostly stranded in the ship basement for three months with four bears, a fact which probably contributes to their sinister appearance. The crossing lasted thirteen days and the ship carried 252 passengers, only thirteen in cabins.

The day after the arrival of the "Wandering Arabs in Lévis", Le Quotidien de Lévis published an article on the nuisance of bears in the city. It stated that the bear performers were French and they had been returning every year for several years. They did not go unnoticed!

1890-07-08 SS BUENOS AYREAN from Glasgow to Québec City

On July 8, 1890, three men with two bears arrived at Quebec. They are difficult to identify, but the discovery of the Liverpool departure manifest facilitated the task.

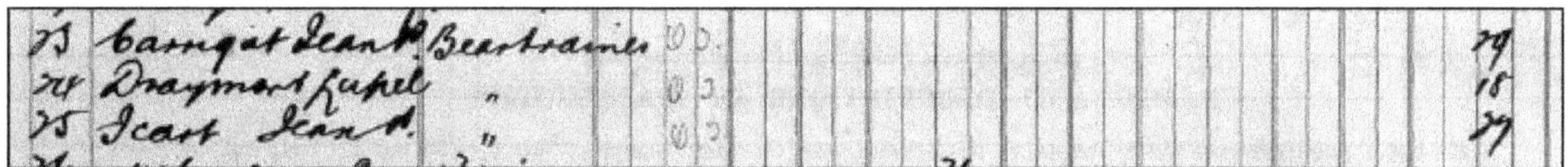

Manifest from Glasgow on June 28, 1890. They are Bear Trainers.

We could identify the men as Jean Pierre MAURY Carregot, Raymond HUGUET Balent and Jean Pierre ICART Cascat.

1890-09-09 SS SIBERIAN from Glasgow to Québec City

This arrival in Quebec of four bear performers in September may have surprised many.

Among the passengers landed at Quebec that day, four men corresponding to numbers 22 to 25 had Ariège-type names. The list of passengers departing from Glasgow dated August 30, 1890, makes it possible to identify them. A rare phenomenon, the nicknames are given and mentioned before the surname and the first name.

This ship stopped in Québec City and then went on to Montreal. In addition to the bear performers, twenty-two Canadian cattle keepers (Cattlemen) traveled on the ship.

The fall being cold in Quebec, one wonders what bear performers were going to do, because at that time of the year, recreational activities were over. One possible explanation is that they immediately went to the south of the United States; another is that they put their bears on board for the winter to work in hotels or restaurants.

1891-05-22 SS LAKE SUPERIOR from Liverpool to Québec City

The four passengers corresponding to number 2394 were found thanks to the departure manifest written up in Liverpool on May 22, 1891. The date of arrival in Montreal and the manifest were not found. Presumably the LAKE SUPERIOR arrived in Quebec between May 29 and June 2, 1891, because at that date several bear performers reported to the Montreal Consulate.

Biography of Paul GALY Tristan

Born on May 13, 1861, in Cominac, he left for the Infantry Regiment in November 1882. He served there until September 1886, then lived in Sète for the next few years. Returning home to Ercé, he followed in the footsteps of his older brother Jean Pierre and became a bear performer.

Provided with a "Carnet de saltimbanque" in 1889, he traveled with six bear showmen to France and England. On March 19, 1890, he was in Southampton. From May to July 1890, the English newspapers mentioned that he showed the bear with other companions in front of Queen Victoria. Indeed, on May 7, 1890, the London newspaper The Pall

Mall Gazette reported that Paul GALY Tristan and Joseph BARAT had their bears dance on the Longwalk leading to Windsor Castle.

In July 1890, Paul GALY returned home, quite proud of his feat before the queen. Still single, after a short period of military drills in the fall of 1890, he returned in 1891. He is in the official census of England in Surrey under his middle name Michel. Four Ariégeois bear performers appear at 10 Middle Street in Croydon in a small boarding house run by an Italian. Jean and Joseph BARAT as well as Raymond and Michel GALY identify themselves as Bear Keepers. Raymond GALY Toou was aboard ship which arrived May 21, 1891.

June 2, 1891, is an important date for Paul GALY Tristan. When reporting to the Montreal Consulate that day, did he realize that this would be the official date of his final arrival in North America? He returned to France only briefly after the death of his father in 1893. His years of bear exhibiting ended when he married Octavie LACHANCE, a native of Quebec, on October 30, 1894, in Québec City. On the marriage certificate, his nickname Tristan is clearly readable.

At the birth of their child Jean Auguste in 1900, the godfather and godmother are Jean RIVIÈRE Miquéou and Jeanne GÉRAUD Rey, two compatriots who appear among the most important peddlers of religious objects from Lourdes. In 1901, the family lived in the St-Roch district of Québec City and Paul GALY worked in the hotel business. Four children are mentioned in the 1901 census: Paul (1895), Jeanne (1897), Marie Ange (1899) and Jean Auguste (1900).

In 1903, the family lived at 36 rue du Roi, and the father was a dyer at J.-A. Paquet, a large manufacturer of fur goods (Source: MARCOTTE Québec Directory).

In 1905, he became a Canadian citizen and everything seemed to go well until the death of his wife Octavie on June 19, 1907, in Montreal. As a widower with four young children, he moved to Montreal. He opened a delicatessen on Notre-Dame Street in Montreal in front of the Commercial Hotel where his Ariège friends had set up their quarters.

In 1908, he married Marie BEAUDIN in Montreal and in 1911, the whole family was living on the 1314 Notre-Dame Street West, in the same building as the deli. They resided there until 1916.

In 1917, Paul and Marie GALY were restaurateurs in Manchester, New Hampshire, at 27 Central Street. They returned to Quebec at the end of the war and settled permanently in Napierville to run another diner place. The children got married in Montreal, and in turn had children. A long, busy life for Paul GALY Tristan ended on August 7, 1933, in Saint-Cyprien, Napierville. His wife moved to Saint-Jean-d'Iberville where she was still on Canada's list of electors in 1940. Several of Paul GALY's descendants now live in Saint-Constant and Verdun.

***

On October 17, 1891, an English newspaper, The Era of London, reported the presence of wrestling bears at Montreal's Sohmer Park. For sure, some bear performers decided to offer different shows, for instance they would fight with the bear or have the bears fight each other. There were many fans in the North American public for this kind of wrestling attraction.

1892-06-27 SS BUENOS AYREAN from Glasgow to Québec City

At numbers 28 and 29, two Ariégeois are on the list, Jean CAUJOLLE and Jos. SOUQUET, they declared themselves Showmen.

1894-07-09 SS LAKE ONTARIO from Liverpool to Montreal

Two Ariégeois named Jean, Jean LOUBET Mantègne and Jean MERLE Ste-Croix Crouzet arrived in Montreal on July 9, 1894. One of them reported to the consulate two days later, but their itinerary that year remains unknown.

1894-08-13 SS LAKE ONTARIO from Liverpool to Québec City

On August 13, at the port of Québec City, many people enjoying a walk by the wharf saw two bear performers arrive. Jean P. DÉGEILH, 25, and Bernard BÉNAZET, 50, clearly identified themselves as Performers with Performing Bear. So they had a bear for two showmen, the normal ratio in this business.

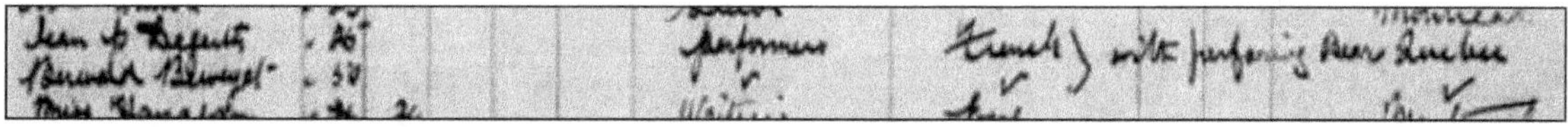

Ship Manifest of the SS LAKE ONTARIO

Biography of Jean Pierre DEGEILH Malet

Born on November 17, 1869, in Cominac, Jean Pierre is one of the bear showmen to make a career in American circuses. Not having appeared in military service in 1889, he was initially considered a "good absentee", was then exempted from the exercise period in 1909 because he was abroad before being finally declared "Rebellious". One then might very well infer he left France at twenty and never returned.

We know that in 1894 he lived in England. From Liverpool, he embarked for Quebec with Bernard BÉNAZET Rebéou, an old showman then fifty years old. They made Fatima, their bear, dance in the Dime Museums and Jean Pierre was noticed by some fairground owners always on the lookout for wild animals' shows. He joined a circus and became a lion tamer under the name of Captain Cardona.

He married Mathilde BÉNAZET Cabos of Ercé in New York in 1907, and they emigrated permanently to the United States. His brother Pierre joined him in America and the two brothers had a career in the circus world always with wild animals – bears, lions, leopards and elephants.

The risks of accidents are numerous in the circus and Jean Pierre DÉGEILH succumbed to wounds on August 9, 1911, in a New York hospital. He is buried in Calumet, Michigan. His last job was that of elephant tamer in 1911 at the Sun Brothers Circus.

From a traveling bear wanderer to the life of lions and elephants tamer, Jean Pierre DÉGEILH lived a very different life than he would have had in his hamlet of Cominac.

***

Ariège bear showmen are not the only ones on the territory.

Other bear performers attempted to exploit the enthusiasm of North Americans for animal shows. On April 30, 1895, a group of about thirty people of Turkish origin, with animals, arrived at the port of Québec City on the SS Sardinian. On the ship manifest, one can see the mention: "Wandering Bear performers, plenty of monkeys".

1896-07-02 SS LAKE WINNIPEG from Liverpool to Québec City

Jean BROUÉ and Jean Pierre BROUÉ, both described as artists with a dancing bear, are the sons of Joseph BROUÉ Samsou who came to Montreal in July 1885 on the SS TORONTO. They are also the nephews of the first bear performer who came to Quebec in 1874, Jean BROUÉ Samsou. The brothers are the second generation in the industry.

1898-06-15 SS LAKE HURON from Liverpool to Québec City

The two bear performers who disembarked in Québec City in June 1898 were veterans. Jean Paul AJAS and Jean Pierre FAUR Croustet shuttled between Ercé and America many times.

Biography of Jean Pierre FAUR Croustet also known as Trataï

Born on September 12, 1874, in La Comanie, a hamlet of Ercé, Tataï undertook this trip just after his military service with Jean Paul AJAS dit Carlot, which will mark the beginning of a long career.

He spent a season in England in 1900 and a second the following year, with three companions, Girons POUECH, Baptiste HUGUET and Pierre BÉNAZET. They resided at 114 Tanners Hill, Deptford, London, identified as Bear Leaders in the 1901 census.

Tataï traveled back and forth between England and the Pyrenees until 1903. That year, he sailed on August 26, for Montreal. In 1905 he was back in Quebec, and on October 28 took the SS TUNISIAN from Québec City to Liverpool. His brother Jean Pierre accompanied him as well as two other Oustois, Louis SIRGANT Béarnès and Alexis ARTAUD Capbertat. They did not return to Oust until November 5, 1905.

In 1906 he was away from home from March to June and in October 1907, he was back in Montreal. After a short absence while back at home in France, in April 1909, he was again passing by Montreal and we have evidence he also returned there in October of the same year.

On November 12, 1910, he arrived in New York on LA LORRAINE coming from Le Havre with Jean SOULÉ, Jacques GÉRAUD and Jean ITTÉ. He joined his brother Baptiste at the PERTHUS Hotel at 235 W 37th Avenue in Manhattan. It is not practical to show the bear in November and this is the explanation given when he told the Montreal Consulate that he was working at the Windsor Hotel. Louis GASTON, a fellow countryman, was then a cook there. In July 1913, he was still in Montreal, but was recalled to military duty by the French government in 1914.

On February 12, 1915, he was taken prisoner in the village of Hurlus, one of the villages surrounding La Marne that were completely destroyed during the war of 1914–1918 and never rebuilt. The communes have been eliminated and absorbed by neighboring ones. He was jailed in Merseburg, a prison camp. He remained there for nearly four years and was released on January 28, 1919, under the armistice. He was sent home on February 11, 1919, on demobilization leave. He is single at the time.

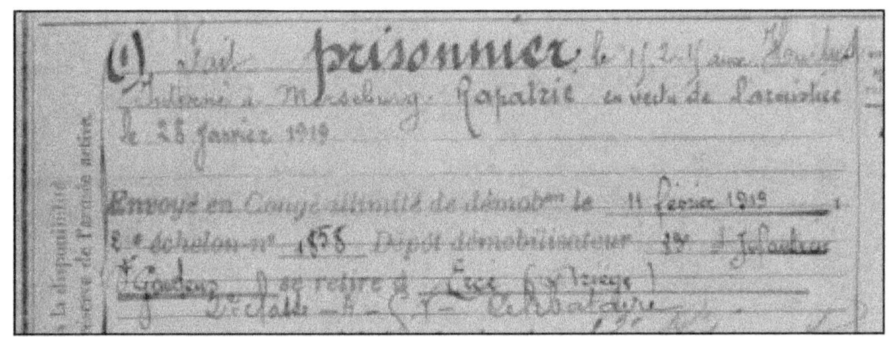

Extract from the military register of Jean Pierre FAUR Croustet, class 1894, number 584.

After good years as a bear performer and others, less good, even horrible during the war, he would now naturally think of settling himself and in October 1919 married Marie PEYRAT Piquet in Ercé. He is forty five, and his bride is twenty-eight.

Tataï lived to be eighty years old and died on May 22, 1954, at La Rivière d'Ercé. Marie PEYRAT lived on until 1977.

1899-05-29 SS RUAPEHU from Liverpool to Québec City

Five bear performers arrived in Québec City. It was possible to identify them by comparing this arrival list with the departure list of May 20, 1899, written up in Liverpool.

The list of RUAPEHU passengers arriving at the port of Québec City on May 29, 1899. Bear Trainer; Italian; 2 Bears; Quebec.

1899-07-20 SS LAKE SUPERIOR from Liverpool to Montreal

Two Ariègeois arrived that day in Montreal, Jean Pierre CAU Basset and Jacques POUMADÉ Paoulétat.

In the passenger list of the SS LAKE SUPERIOR, Jean CAU claims to be a hairdresser and Jacques POUMADÉ, a barber. These mentions of Hairdresser and Barber as trades are surprising because both individuals are known bear performers. In the list of passengers departing Liverpool on July 8, they describe themselves as Travelers.

***

Dancing Bears on early American Silent Movies

Thomas Edison (1847–1931), the famous American inventor of the light bulb and the phonograph, shot two small films on the theme of bear performers in 1899. The first titled "Trick Bears" features bears dressed in skirts and trinkets dancing in circles guided by their masters.

The second "Fun in camp" filmed in Orange, New Jersey, features a group of soldiers and nurses who are having fun watching young children riding on the backs of the bears moving as if horses. The scene is set in an infantry camp of the US Army.

Chapter 5

The years 1900 to 1914 and the end of the epic

In the consular inscriptions mentioned in the military registers of the canton of Oust, several bear performers declared to be passing through or living in Quebec in the years 1900 to 1903. These bear performers arrived in the United States and crossed the border into Canada. A contract involving the sale of a bear (in fact half ownership of a bear) was signed in Montreal in September 1903, at the Hotel Commercial which was a common gathering place for bear showmen in Montreal.

From 1905 to 1911, four ships delivered fifteen bear performers. In 1906 a ship left a record number of eight bear performers in Montreal.

On reading these men's journeys, we discover an industry that is losing steam under the weight of the bans of the various cities and that will undergo a fatal blow on the early stages of the Great War of 1914–1918 and with the general mobilization of the French bear performers that will ensue.

Although for this period, we see ship arrivals starting from 1905, several clues confirm that the industry was alive and well in the years 1900–1904.

First, the consular inscriptions mention the presence of several bear performers: Jean RUFFÉ Caillaou (1900), Jacques GÉRAUD Despagne (1901), Joseph SOULÉ Espagnol (1902) and in 1903, nine bear performers reported to the consulates of Québec City and Montreal—Bernard ROGALLE Clar, Alexis ARTAUD Capbertat, Jean Pierre CABAUP Couartou, Jean FOUNEAU Buharou, Alfred ROGALLE Péou, Pierre ROGALLE Péou, Vincent ROZÈS Barlabé, Jean Pierre FAUR Croustet and Girons ICART Palot.

The discovery of a bear contract, as this kind of contract was called, signed in Montreal in September 1903, confirms the vitality of the industry.

An interesting Bear contract:

"Commercial Hotel, Maurice DURRACQ, owner, September 14, 1903. The contract signed in Montreal by Maurice DURRACQ for Jacques FAUR Don provides the buyer with half a bear for the sum of 300 francs".

It was not uncommon for bear drivers to share a trained bear, which they called the "shared bear". In such a case, both men could show the bear together or take on one season each. So, the bear was boarded until the second owner could take over.

1905-05-20 SS LAKE ERIE from Liverpool to Québec City

On May 20, 1905, two ROGALLE brothers, Paul MERLE and Pierre CAU disembarked. They pretended to be lion tamers. This seems suspicious, as these four men are traditional bear showmen, men walking from town to town with trained bears. The answer to this dilemma came after the discovery of a list of passengers from Liverpool on May 9, 1905. Our four friends are now Travelers, so their job had evolved during the crossing. It is assumed that if the bear performers did not have the animals with them, they could invent the trade that gave them importance or it would simply be an error by the attendant.

1905-06-30 SS LAKE MANITOBA from Liverpool to Québec City

At number 6007, Pierre ROGALLE and Jean GÉRAUD declared they practiced the trade of Touring Bear Performer.

1906-06-08 SS PHILADELPHIAN from Liverpool to Montreal

Eight bear performers landed in Montreal on June 8, 1906. The number of bears accompanying them is not specified, but their job description as "Conductor of Livestock" suggests a bad translation of "animal driver", expression often used in the industry. The reference address is that of the DURRACQ hotel on the 1364 Notre-Dame Street West. The first two passengers: Jean GÉRAUD and Pierre GÉRAUD are single while the six others: Baptiste ROGALLE, Henri PIQUEMAL and his brother Auguste PIQUEMAL, Joseph ROGALLE, Pierre SIRGANT and André SIRGANT are married.

***

On December 26, 1906, Le Quotidien de Lévis reported that a man with two bears was staying at the Bégin hotel in Lévis between Christmas and New Year's Day. His name was PONCELLE according to the article, surely a PONSOLLE of Ercé difficult to identify, because traveling bear performer named PONSOLLE were numerous in America in those years.

1911-10-06 SS CORINTHIAN from Le Havre to Montreal

Only one bear performer is aboard this ship in 1911, Jean Pierre ROGALLE Pétiou. During the war, he worked for the American circus Sun Brothers. His brother Bernard joined him there in 1917.

The industry was running out of steam and the war put to an end the comings and goings of these public entertainers.

The end of the epic

The Great War of 1914-18 put an end to the 40-year-old Ariège dancing bear industry. Since 1900, some signals indicated a decline in this dynamic group.

Towns and villages showed intolerance in the form of bans and arrests with respect to traveling shows with animals. In 1911, it was England's turn to ban them. As Liverpool was still the hub for naval crossing, it detracted from the bear performers' movements to America. These men though, could still make the crossing via Le Havre or Bordeaux but they still had to travel to the American ports which also stiffened their admission criteria.

Moreover, the French authorities were not happy with these migrations, which had the effect of depopulating certain villages.

Then came the Order of general mobilization of August 2, 1914, all the French, even those abroad, were called to arms.

Joseph ANDREU Pascoualet, the last bear performer from Ariège, died in France in 1966. Alfred ROGALLE Péou was the last immigrant bear showman in Canada. He died in Montreal in 1963.

Chapter 6

The photo album of bear showmen in North America

Photo 1: Two Ariège bear performers and two bears. Nicolet, Quebec. Circa 1910.

The bears hold the "bastoun" to proudly imitate the shepherd. This scene is part of the Ariège ritual. The tamer in the foreground could be André GÉRAUD Parracha about fifty years old, which would set the scene in the 1900s.

Photo 2: Bears at Carrollcroft Gardens. Circa 1902.

Two bear performers on the left guiding two standing bears mimicking the shepherd and a third performer leaning holding a bear behind him. Spectators are from the Colby family and guests. The scene is behind Colby Manor in Stanstead near the Canada-US border.

Photo 3: Bear standing on his hind legs and two showmen, Charlottetown, Prince Edward Island. Circa 1894.

Curious people admire the bear standing and its two showmen.

Photo 4: People watching tame bears in front of Indian River Hotel, Rockledge, Florida. Circa 1900.

Two bear performers with their animals roam under the palm trees of this central Florida City. The bear on the left has an enormous lump on its spine. The second showman carrying a bugle is about to give a show. The crowd looks rather warmly dressed for a Florida setup indicating a winter performance most likely.

Photo 5: Performing Bear, Pub. by R.B. Honey, Dexter, Michigan. Circa 1910.

This crowd in Dexter is really intrigued by the behavior of the bear which exhibits its muscles in the manner of a bodybuilder. It stands surprisingly straight and his showman is very calm. He carries a bugle, an instrument used to rouse crowds.

Photo 6: Dancing Bear, Sedgley Bull Ring, Sedgley, England.

The standing bear is holding the "bastoun" with his upper paws, he seems very comfortable standing. His leader is on the left and slightly back, a trick used to make the bear appear bigger.

Photo credits

Photo 1 : Archives of the Nicolet Seminary, F085-P9002.
Photo 2: Colby-Curtis Museum and Stanstead Historical Society, Quebec.
Photo 3: Jim Hornby, Bear Facts, The History and Folklore of Island Bears, Part 2, The Island Magazine, 1987.
Photo 4: State Archives of Florida, Florida Memory.
Photo 5: Beauty and the Beast: Human Animal Relations as revealed in Real Photo Postcards 1905–1935, Arnold Arluke and Robert Bogdan.
Photo 6: Sedgley Local History Society.

Conclusion

In the 19th century, bear showing was a dangerous job that allowed you to see the world and to escape poverty.

Under all sorts of names, these men of Ariège worked in Quebec and elsewhere in America. Some had a career, others used their craft to earn money to buy land and get married.

Recruitment in this industry was by family, neighbors and hamlet and the trade was spread over two generations.

The tamer industry suffered a real decline when the Great War of 1914–1918 broke out. French citizens on a trip had to go back and report for war and Quebec citizens no longer were in a mood to enjoy distractions.

The bear performers brought their bears back to the fold and kept them on their land. Some sold their bears to circuses or zoos and the most original, Jean Pierre FAUR Croustet aka Dataï, sold his animal to the Natural History Museum of New York.

Although most bear performers were temporary migrants for a season or two–and sometimes more– some settled in Quebec for good. After their bear performer years, they worked as farmers, cooks and tradesmen. Thus, if you come across a BROUÉ in the Outaouais and Montreal regions, a ROGALLE in Montreal, a RIEUX in the Outaouais, a CLASTRES in Sorel, a GALY in Napierville, Saint-Constant or Verdun, a BACQUÉ in the Québec City region or an ICART in Pont-Rouge, Tewkesbury or Québec City, you can say that they are descendants of a race of men and women with uncommon resilience and inventiveness.

The story of these bear performers, this merely forgotten profession, earned the right to be told. An episode of forty years from 1874 to 1914 that deserves its place in the North American history.

□□□

References

Directories

Annuaire Marcotte de Québec (1903).

Liste des électeurs du Canada, 1935 à 1980.

Lovell Directory, Montréal, 1921 à 1963.

U.S. City Directories : New York City, Troy (1916, 1938 et 1940) et Albany (1927).

Articles

Clairoux, Jacques M.. *Le théâtre ambulant et ses amuseurs publics*, Cap-aux-Diamants : la revue d'histoire du Québec, n° 35, 1993, p. 46-49.

De Lottinville, Peter. *Joe Beef of Montreal : Working-Class. Culture and the Tavern, 1869-1889*, Labour/Le Travailleur, 8/9, 1981-1982, p. 9-40.

Deschamps, Jean-Louis (Aulus, Ariège), Françoise Lewis (Montréal) et Louise Pagé (Montréal). *Les montreurs d'ours de l'Ariège,* La mémoire du Garbet, bulletin spécial, 2ᵉ semestre 2011, 52 pages. (Répertoire des 600 montreurs d'ours de l'industrie).

Etchelecou, André. *Ariège, la fin d'un pays?*, Université de Bordeaux, France, 1981, p.307-321. Consulté sur http://www.erudit.org

Fléchet, Jean. *Le montreur d'ours*, Atelier du Gué, France, 1997.

Hornby, Jim. *Bear Facts, The History and Folklore of Island Bears*, Part Two, The Island Magazine, 1987, p. 27-31.

Lalumière, Antoinette. *La danse de l'ours*, consulté le 20 mai 2009 sur http://histoiredeweedon.info

Lewis, Françoise. *Des montreurs d'ours à Montréal*, La Mémoire du Garbet, bulletin no 34, 2008, p.41.

Pagé, Louise. *La diaspora d'Oust à Layrac,* bulletin de La Généalogie en Agenais, Agen, juillet 2014.
Le destin américain des Broué Cabillot d'Arrous, La Mémoire du Garbet, bulletin no 42, 2012, p.20-26.
Les Broué d'Amérique, L'Outaouais généalogique, vol. XXXIV, numéro 2, 2012, p. 88-91.

Penisson, Bernard, *Un siècle d'immigration française au Canada (1881-1980)*, Revue européenne de migrations internationales, Volume 2, Numéro 2, p.111-125.

Times Record, Troy, NY, *Necrologies*, 12 juin 1945, 20 juin 1955, 11 mai 1974, 24 avril 1947, 9 mars 1950, 1er et 3 novembre 1969, 13 juillet 1972.

Savard, Pierre. *Les Canadiens français vus par les Consuls de France à Québec et Montréal de 1859 à 1900*, Revue d'histoire de l'Amérique française, vol.21, no 2, 1967, p.217-229.

Sutteret, Jean et Jean-Michel Goux. *Évolution de la consanguinité en France de 1926 à 1958 avec des données récentes détaillées*, Population, 17e année, 1962, France, p.683-702.

Vigroux, Sophie. *L'aventure des oursaillers*, entrevue avec Gabriel Bénazet d'Ercé, La dépêche du Midi, Toulouse, 17 avril 2011.

Vineberg Robert. *Quebec City – The forgotten Port of entry*, Canadian Immigration Historical Society Newsletter, Issue 59, September 2010.

Conferences ans interviews

Pagé Louise. *Les Ariégeois du Canton d'Oust au Canada 1874 – 1914*, conférence à la mairie d'Oust, 27 mai 2013.

Pagé, Louise, *Entrevue sur les montreurs d'ours réalisée* par Johane Despins, ICI Radio Canada Première, Dessine-moi un dimanche, 20 juillet 2014.

Sauvée, Michel. *Une particularité pyrénéenne : la prédominance de la « maison »*, Conférence dans le cadre des Journées nationales de

Généalogie de l'Entraide généalogique du Midi Toulousain, Toulouse, 2 octobre 2004.

Films

Fun in camp, 27 novembre 1899, Thomas Edison, Library of Congress Motion Picture, Broadcasting and Recorded Sound Division Washington, D. C. 20540 USA. Consulté sur http://www.loc.gov/item/00694212/

Le montreur d'ours, 1996, Francis Fourcou, 35 mm couleur — 97 minutes, France.

L'orsalhèr, 1984, Jean Fléchet, 107 minutes. Les dialogues sont en occcitan.

Trick Bears, 1899, Thomas Edison, Library of Congress Motion Picture, Broadcasting and Recorded Sound Division Washington, D. C. 20540 USA dcu [consulté sur http://www.loc.gov/item/00694321/].

Books
France

De Marliave, Olivier. *Histoire de l'ours dans les Pyrénées*, Éditions sud-ouest, France, 2008.

Decossaux, Marie-Lou. *Sapou, Colporteur de l'Ariège au temps des montreurs d'ours*, Éditions de Provence, France, 1995, 222 pages. Éditions Le pas de l'oiseau, à paraître 2015.

Gastou, François-Régis. *Sur les traces des montreurs d'ours des Pyrénées et d'ailleurs*, Éditions Loubatières, France, p.128-137; 183.

Géraud Guillaume Parracha, *Par les sentiers et les sillons*, Oust, France, 2001, 425 pages. (à compte d'auteur).

Hausmann, *Mémoires du Baron Haussmann*, Paris, 1890, p.165-167.

Lewis, Françoise. *Le vicomte de Couserans et les irréductibles seixois*, Éditions Lacour, France, 2010, 245 pages.

Moulis, Adelin. *En Ariège : la vie de nos ancêtres*, Éditions Lacour, 1985, 162 pages.

Saliès, Pierre et Régis Loubès. *Quand l'Ariège changea de siècle*, Milan, 1982, 511 pages.

Québec et Ontario

Bliss, Michael. *Plague : A Story of Smallpox in Montreal*, Harper Collection, Toronto, 1991, 306 pages.

Dupont, Jean-Claude. *Coutumes et superstitions.* Éd. J.-C. Dupont, Sainte-Foy, Québec, 64 pages. (inclut une peinture intitulée Le montreur d'ours peinte par l'auteur en 1978).

Fournier, Marcel. *Les Français au Québec 1765-1865, Un mouvement migratoire méconnu*, Éditions du Septentrion, Québec, 1995, 386 pages.

Lalonde Cloutier, Margot. *Notre-Dame-de-la-Paix 1902-2002*, Éditions de la Petite-Nation, Québec, 2002, 83 pages.

Lewis, Françoise. *Montreurs d'ours en Australie et Nouvelle-Zélande*, Montréal, 2010, 159 pages et *Montreurs d'ours en Angleterre*, Montréal, 170 pages, 2013. (à compte d'auteur).

Pomerleau, Jeanne, *Métiers ambulants d'autrefois*, Guérin Littérature, Québec, 1990, 467 pages.
Le montreur d'ours, Éditions du Méridien, 1988, 104 pages.

Potvin, Damase, *Le montreur d'ours*, nouvelle, 1927.

Ships manifests
Listes de passagers pour les ports de Québec et de Montréal 1865-1900. Consultée sur www.collectionscanada.gc.ca

Listes de passagers canadiens, 1865 à 1935, listes des passages frontaliers : du Canada aux États-Unis, 1895 à 1956 et des passages frontaliers : des États-Unis au Canada, 1908 à 1935. Consultées sur www.ancestry.ca

Listes de passagers d'Ellis Island, à partir de 1892 consultées sur www.ellisisland.org

Liste de passagers de Castle Garden, à partir de 1855, consultées sur www.castlegarden.org

Liste des passagers en partance, Royaume Uni, port de Liverpool, 1890-1960.

Theses

Marie-Lou Decossaux, *Des montreurs d'ours aux restaurateurs new-yorkais : trois générations de migrants ariégeois*, mémoire, Centre d'études nord-américaines, E.H.E.S.S., Paris, 1982. Contribution de Vincent Rozès, maire d'Oust, France, 2013.

Notaries

Extraits des greffes des notaires ariégeois : Me Auzies, Me Dégeilh, Me Géraud, Me Peyras et Me Vidal ainsi que le juge de paix Auguste Bousquet.

Notaire Antoine RABY, Saint-André-Avellin, archives consultées sur
http : //www.banq.qc.ca

République française, ministère de l'Intérieur, Direction de la Sûreté
générale, 3e Bureau, *Émigration-Canada, circulaire no 90 à l'intention des
Préfets*, Paris, 21 août 1911.

Registers

Archives départementales de l'Ariège (09), de la Haute-Garonne (31) et du
Lot-et-Garonne (46) :
http://archives.ariege.fr/
http://archives.haute-garonne.fr/
http://archives.lot.fr/

Archives de l'Entraide généalogique midi toulousain disponibles sur
http : //www.geneabank.org

Archives nationales de France : https://www.siv.archives-
nationales.culture.gouv.fr

Banque de données : www.ancestry.ca; www.ancestry.com;
www.ancestry.uk et www.ancestry.fr

Blogue de Cominac par Roger Carrère :

http://cominac1906.skyrock.com/8.html, Roger Carrère

Compilation des Recrutements militaires du canton d'Oust (09) de 1857 à 1899, Claudie Dussert, France.

Liste nominative des insoumis ayant plus de 45 ans à la date du 1er août 1913 et qui doivent être rayés des contrôles d'insoumission, en exécution de la loi d'amnistie du 31 juillet 1911. Bureau de St-Gaudens.

Mémoire des hommes, Ministère de la Défense, France : http://www.memoiredeshommes.sga.defense.gouv.fr/

*Registre No 1 pour l'inscription des demandes de Carnets de saltimbanque*s, Exécution de la Circulaire du 6 janvier 1863. Ariège.

Registres de l'état civil (originaux). Mairies d'Oust, Ercé et Ustou, Ariège.

Registres des baptêmes, mariages et sépultures de Seix, compilation de Jean Pierre Verdier : http://genealogie.seix.free.fr

Registres criminels, 1791-1892, Angleterre et Wales, comté de Cumberland.

Census

BROUÉ, Jean, Recensement canadien de 1891, page 33 de 52; Recensement canadien de 1901, Microfilm no T -6526, District 160 – Labelle, sous-district W5 – St. Andre-Avellin, page 4 et Recensement canadien de 1921, Montréal, sous-district 13, Mercier and Maisonneuve Ward.

Recensements du Canada (1891, 1901, 1911 et 1921) consultés sur http://www.collectionscanada.gc.ca et www.ancestry.ca

Ontario Genealogical Society, archives consultées sur http://www.ogspi.on.ca

U.S. Census (1910), Glens Falls, État de New York.

U.S. Census (1930), Troy, État de New York.

Index of ships

Index of Bear Handlers

Names and year(s) of arrival

A

AJAS Jean Paul Carlet dit Palot 1898

AJAS Guilhaume Pégou 1881

B

BACQUE Pierre Cubat 1874

BACQUÉ Paul dit Sant 1890

BACQUÉ Jean Niveille 1890

BADIÉ Jean Lebet 1890

BARAT Baptiste 1890

BARAT Baptiste Padié 1886

BÉNAZET Jacques Pierre Burrat 1881 et 1885

BÉNAZET Jean Baptiste Cabos 1877

BÉNAZET Baptiste Couserans 1890

BÉNAZET Bernard Rébéou 1894

BROUÉ Jean Cabillot 1885

BROUÉ Jean Samsou 1874 et 1899

BROUÉ Jean Samsou (neveu) 1896

BROUÉ Jean Pierre Samsou 1896

BROUÉ Joseph Samsou 1885

C

CAU Jean Pierre Basset 1887 et 1899

CAU Pierre de Cau 1905

CAU Pierre de Cau Oueillaret 1887

CAU Paul Ritouret Talar 1890

CAUBET Jean Pierre Lareille Moumat 1887

CAUBET Jean Pierre Lareille Moumat (cadet) 1891

CAUJOLLE Jean Baptiste Bert 1892

CAUJOLLE Jean Lapaille 1881 et 1885

CAUJOLLE Pierre Lapaille 1885

CAUJOLLE Jean Ségadou 1890

D

DÉGEILH Jean Courate 1887

DÉGEILH Jean Pierre Courate 1886

DÉGEILH Jean Pierre Malet 1894

DÉGEILH Pierre Courate Simoun 1890

DURAN J. Luc 1885

E-F

ESPERTE Jean Pierre Mengrille 1880

FAUR Jean Pierre Croustet dit Rataï 1898

G

GALY Raymond Toou 1891

GALY Paul Tristan 1891

GÉRAUD Jean Chez 1906

GÉRAUD Pierre Chez 1906

GÉRAUD Joseph Dardet 1890

GÉRAUD Jean Lourette 1890

GÉRAUD Jean Mierrou 1905

GÉRAUD André Parracha 1881, 1885 et 1899

GÉRAUD Jean Pierre Parracha 1899

H

HUGUET Raymond Balent 1890

HUGUET Baptiste Lagusat 1899

I-L

ICART Jean Pierre Cascat 1890

ICART Jacques Moumat 1881

ICART Jean Moumat 1889

ICART Baptiste Palot 1887

ICART Joseph Sarrabille 1887

LOUBET Jean Mantègne 1894

M

MAURY Baptiste Bourriquet 1881

MAURY Jean Pierre Carregot 1890

MAURY Jean Roch 1890

MERLE Jean Ste Croix Crouzet 1894

MERLE Paul Ste Croix Crouzet 1905

P

PERTHUS Jacquet Vincent 1890

PEYRAT Jean Mathielas 1880

PEYRAT Baptiste Piquet 1890

PIQUEMAL Auguste Coulinet 1906

PIQUEMAL Henri Coulinet 1906

POUECH Joseph Faillet 1890

POUECH Jacques Gradémil 1890

POUECH Jean Jouanou 1890

POUMADÉ Jacques Paoulétat 1899

PUJOL Joseph Sabatou 1881

R

RIEU Jean Baptiste Baychet 1886

RIVIÈRE P. 1877

ROGALLE Bernard Clar 1881

ROGALLE Maria Clar 1889

ROGALLE Pierre Clar Caquet 1905

ROGALLE Bernard Clar Jacole Pétiou 1905

ROGALLE Jean Clar Jacole Pétiou 1905

ROGALLE Jean Pierre Clar Jacole Pétiou 1911

ROGALLE Jean Baptiste Clar Peruc 1891

ROGALLE Pierre Labat 1890

ROGALLE Joseph Luciat Gudanes 1906

ROGALLE Pierre Luciat Gudanes 1899

ROGALLE Baptiste Méringuet 1890

ROGALLE Baptiste Paloubart 1906

S

SERVAT Bernard Sansouci 1886

SERVAT Jean Pierre Sansouci 1877

SERVAT Jean Baptiste Tarrieu 1877

SIRGANT André Béarnès 1906

SIRGANT Pierre Bessou 1906

SOUQUET Jean Malet 1889

SOUQUET Joseph Péguesse 1892

About the author:

Born in Montreal, Louise Pagé, M.Math., MBA, has an ancestor Jean Broué, who, in 1885, left his Pyrenean village with his own bear to come to Canada. In this book, through various documents and pictures, she introduces us to these Bear Handlers who emigrated from France to Canada before World War I, some who, like Jean Broué, stayed in North America for good. Building on the itinerary of her ancestor Broué, we will discover more than ninety showmen performing with their dancing bears on the roads of yesteryear. They are introduced through documents attesting their arrival and their wanderings are related in the form of brief biographies, notes and anecdotes based on important personal documentation like of—ship manifests, circus data, newspapers, census, church and military records—excerpts from these records illustrate the book. What surprises us in the history of these showmen is that everything happened in a short time frame at the turn of the 20th century. Even more surprisingly, these circus men all came from three small neighboring villages in the French Pyrenees.

Contact: ellepage@sympatico.ca